MUSICAL
INSTRUMENTS
OF THE WORLD

Keyboards

Barrie Carson Turner
Illustrated by John See

Belitha Press

First published in the UK in 2000 by
Belitha Press Limited
London House, Great Eastern Wharf,
Parkgate Road, London SW11 4NQ

Editor: Russell McLean
Designer: Zoe Quayle
Picture researcher: Juliet Duff
Educational consultant: Celia Pardaens

ISBN 1 84138 115 2

Printed in Singapore

British Library Cataloguing in Publication Data
for this book is available from the British Library.

10 9 8 7 6 5 4 3 2 1

Picture acknowledgements:
J. Allan Cash: 4-5, 14, 21. Eye Ubiquitous: 23.
Courtesy of Fenton House/National Trust: 7, 13, 15, 18, 27.
The Lebrecht Collection: 22 Graham Salter/Courtesy of Finchcocks.
Redferns: 10 Odile Noel; 25 David Redfern. Mark Solomon: 19, 26.
Tony Stone Images: 11. John Walmsley: 6, 17.

Contents

Musical

Musical instruments are played in every country of the world. There are many thousands of different instruments of all shapes and sizes. They are often divided into four groups: strings, brass, percussion and woodwind.

Percussion instruments are struck (hit), shaken or scraped to make their sound. Brass and woodwind instruments are blown to make their sound. String instruments sound when their strings vibrate.

instruments

This book is about keyboard instruments.
Keyboard instruments sound when their keys
are pressed. The keys on a piano operate small
hammers. The hammers strike the piano strings.
On a church organ, the keys release air that
is forced through the organ pipes. The keys
on an electronic keyboard operate switches.
The switches make the instrument sound.

You can read about 18 different
keyboard instruments in this book.
There is a picture of each instrument
and a photograph of it being played.
On pages 30 and 31 you will find
a list of useful words to help you
understand more about music.

Upright piano

The upright piano takes its name from its shape. The strings are positioned vertically inside the wooden body. When the keys are pressed, small hammers strike the strings. There are two or three pedals at the bottom of the piano. They are worked by the player's feet, and add variety to the sound of the instrument.

music stand

lid

The upright piano is designed to fit neatly against a wall.

keys

pedals

Fortepiano

Fortepiano is the name given to an early piano. The illustration shows the very first piano. It was invented and built by an Italian keyboard maker, Bartolomeo Cristofori, almost 300 years ago. The strings were struck by small, square hammers with leather tips.

lid

strings

keyboard

The sound of the fortepiano is similar to the modern piano, but much less powerful.

Celesta

keys

The celesta (sel-es-ta) looks like a small piano. It was invented in 1886 by Auguste Mustel, a French instrument maker. Inside the wooden body are small steel plates. When the keys are pressed, tiny hammers hit the plates. This makes an attractive ringing sound.

The Russian composer Tchaikovsky wrote an important part for the celesta in the *Dance of the Sugar-Plum Fairy*. This piece of music appears in his ballet *Nutcracker*.

music stand

lid

sustaining pedal

wooden body

Underneath each plate is a small hollow box called a resonator. This gives each plate a rich sound when it is struck. At the base of the celesta is the sustaining pedal. The player presses the pedal down to make the steel plates ring for longer.

Melodica

The melodica makes a sound similar to the mouth organ. Inside the plastic case are thin pieces of metal called reeds. When air is blown across the reeds they vibrate, making the instrument sound. The player holds the melodica like a recorder, and presses the keys to make the notes.

plastic body

keys

blow hole

This unusual melodica has a miniature piano keyboard built into it.

Accordion

Inside the accordion are many thin pieces of metal called reeds. Players squeeze the bellows in and out to force air across the reeds. This makes the accordion sound. The right hand plays the melody on the keyboard. The left hand presses in the finger buttons to make the bass notes and chords.

bellows

keyboard

finger buttons

The accordion hangs by a neck strap, leaving both hands free to play.

Harpsichord

The harpsichord has been played since the 1400s. For 350 years it was the most common keyboard instrument. The harpsichord could make loud sounds, so it was ideal for playing in an orchestra. Today the harpsichord is only used to perform very old music.

keyboards

pedals

lid

When the keys are pressed, small quills pluck the strings. A quill is the hard spine of a bird's feather. There are two or more strings to each note. The player chooses how many strings are played by pulling out a small lever called a stop. Using all the strings makes the music loud. Using fewer strings makes the music softer.

Big harpsichords often have more than one keyboard. Each set of keys makes a different sound. This musician is playing on two keyboards at once.

strings

Electronic organ

The electronic organ usually has at least two keyboards. These are called manuals. A row of pedals is played by the feet. The player presses switches, called stops, to make special sounds. Drum and percussion rhythms are programmed into the organ. They accompany the tune played by the organist.

music stand

keyboards (manuals)

stops

swell pedal

foot pedals for lowest notes

The organist presses the stops to give each manual its own sound.

Virginal

The virginal was first played almost 500 years ago. Some virginals are simple boxes which are played on a table. Others have their own legs. When the keys are pressed, small quills pluck the strings.

lid

keyboard

strings

The keyboard of the virginal is quite small. The body must be large to hold the long strings.

Grand piano

The body of the grand piano is long and flat, and shaped like a wing. The strings inside the piano are laid out in the shape of a harp.

music stand

keys

pedals

strings

The grand piano is too large for most houses. You will often see it at a concert. Here a grand piano is part of a school band.

lid

When the keys are pressed, small hammers strike the strings. The thick strings to the left of the player sound low notes. The thin strings to the right sound high notes. Three pedals at the bottom of the piano control the sound of the instrument. They make the notes rich and strong or soft and gentle. When the piano is played in a large hall, the lid can be opened to make the sound louder.

Clavichord

The clavichord was the first keyboard instrument that people played at home, about 500 years ago. It is shaped like a long box, and is often played on a table. When the keys are pressed, small metal blades, called tangents, strike the strings. This is similar to the hammers striking the strings on a piano.

keys

lid

The sound of the clavichord is soft and delicate, which made it ideal for playing at home.

strings

18

Player piano

The player piano is automatic – so it needs no performer! It is worked by paper rolls which are punched with holes. As the roll turns, the holes act like a code, telling the instrument which notes to play. The illustration shows an early electric model. Other models are worked by bellows. The player piano can also be played like an ordinary piano. Another name for this instrument is pianola.

paper roll

electric light

music stand

keys

pedals

This player piano is worked by bellows. The musician presses them with his feet. The bellows blow air to turn the paper rolls.

Keyboards

Today the word
keyboards is used to
mean electronic keyboards
of any type. There are many
different shapes and sizes
of instrument. Some
of them are small
enough to carry
under your arm.

Keyboards have
been used in rock,
pop and dance
bands for over
25 years. Musicians
often play several
different keyboards
during a performance.

display
screen

keys

control
buttons

Modern keyboards can copy
the sounds made by many other
instruments. These include traditional
keyboard instruments such as the piano
and the organ. More unusual sounds
played by a keyboard include
ambulance sirens, ringing telephones
and even buzzing mosquitoes!

The electronic keyboard
is one of the most
exciting instruments
to play. It can copy
the sound of a
complete orchestra.

Dulcitone

The first dulcitone (dul-si-tone) was made 200 years ago. Its original name was the tuning fork piano. Inside the wooden case is a row of metal bars. Each bar is shaped like the letter U. When the keys are pressed, small hammers strike the bars. Each bar sounds a different note.

lid

music stand

keys

pedal

wooden case

The sound made by the dulcitone is soft and mellow.

Hurdy-gurdy

The hurdy-gurdy rests on a player's lap or hangs by a neck strap. The strings are sounded by a wheel coated with a substance called rosin. This helps the wheel to grip the strings and make a strong sound. When the keys are pressed, small wooden blades push against the strings to make the notes.

strings

tuning pegs

wheel

keyboard

handle

A hurdy-gurdy player turns the wheel with one hand and plays the tune on the keyboard with the other.

Church organ

The organ has been played for more than 2000 years. It is the largest and loudest of all musical instruments. The first organs were pumped by hand. Modern instruments have electric pumps. A church organ has several sets of pipes. On a large instrument some pipes are as long as ten metres. Long pipes sound low notes. Short pipes sound high notes.

keyboards (manuals)

stops

foot pedals for lowest notes

pipes

When an organ is played, air is forced upwards through a pipe. The air strikes the sharp edge of an opening, cut into the metal. This makes the pipe sound. An organ usually has two or three keyboards. They are called manuals. Levers called stops are pushed in or pulled out to lead the air from one set of pipes to another.

The organist gives each manual its own sound by pulling out or pushing in the stops.

25

Digital piano

The digital piano has no strings. Each note is a recording taken from a real piano. When a key is pressed, the note sounds from a loudspeaker under the keyboard. The digital piano can copy the sounds of many other instruments. It can also record music played on it.

control panel

music stand

keys

pedals

The digital piano is played in exactly the same way as an ordinary piano.

Spinet

Spinet

Before the invention of the piano the spinet was one of the most popular home keyboard instruments. It works in the same way as its bigger cousin, the harpsichord. When the keys are pressed, tiny quills pluck the strings. This makes a quiet tinkling sound. A spinet cannot be played loudly.

strings

lid

Spinets were often beautifully decorated, which made them popular as furniture.

keys

Harmonium

The harmonium makes a sound similar to an organ. It contains many thin pieces of metal called reeds. Another name for the harmonium is reed organ.

At the base of the instrument are two bellows. Players press them in turn with their feet. The bellows pump air across the reeds, which vibrate to make the harmonium sound.

stops

keys

bellows

Above the keyboard is a row of levers called stops. Each stop may be pulled out or pushed in. This directs the air to different sets of reeds to produce a variety of sounds.

This small harmonium is from India. It is played sitting on the floor. The musician works the bellows with his left hand and plays the tune with his right hand.

Words to

accompany To play music alongside a singer or another player who has the tune.

bass notes The lowest notes.

beat The steady pulse of the music.

bellows The part of an instrument that holds air. When a player squeezes the bellows, air is forced through the instrument to make it sound.

chords Groups of notes played together.

concert A performance by players or singers in front of an audience.

family (of instruments) Instruments that are similar to each other.

keyboard The row of keys on a keyboard instrument.

keys The small levers that a keyboard player presses to make the instrument sound.

manual An organ keyboard.

melody A tune.

musician Someone who plays an instrument or sings.

orchestra A large group of musicians playing together.

pedal Any part of an instrument worked by the player's foot.

percussion A family of instruments that are struck, shaken or scraped to make their sound.

performer Someone who plays or sings to other people.

pipe One of the metal or wooden tubes that make up an organ.

remember

quill The hard spine of a bird's feather.

reed A tiny, thin piece of metal or cane that vibrates when air is blown over it. Reeds make the sound in some keyboard instruments.

resonators Hollow boxes underneath the metal plates of a celesta. They make the sound of the instrument louder and more rounded.

rhythm A rhythm is made by the beat of the music, and by how long and short the notes are.

rock A type of pop music which often has a strong beat.

rosin A substance that is rubbed on to the bows of string instruments and the wheel of a hurdy-gurdy to help them grip the strings.

solo A piece played or sung by one player or singer.

stops Levers or knobs which change the sound of some keyboard instruments, such as an organ.

strike To hit the strings of an instrument.

sustaining pedal A lever operated by the foot which allows the notes of a keyboard instrument to sound for longer.

swell pedal A lever on an organ which increases the loudness of the instrument.

tangents Small metal blades that strike the strings of a clavichord.

vibrate The fast shaking of an object such as a string or a reed. Organ reeds vibrate when air is blown over them.

Index